G000275732

	INFORMATION & ABBREVIATIONS	2
	INTRODUCTION	3
Walk No 1	CROOKHAM & DOGMERSFIELD 4 Miles	4
Walk No 2	BEACON HILL & EWSHOT 4 Miles	6
Walk No 3	BRAMSHOT & MINLEY 4 Miles	8
Walk No 4	ITCHEL MILL SPRINGS 4 Miles	10
Walk No 5	CRONDAL 4 Miles	12
Walk No 6	BARLEY MOW & CROOKHAM 4 Miles	14
Walk No 7	WINCHFIELD & DOGMERSFIELD CHURCHES 5 Miles	18
Walk No 8	ELVETHAM 3½ Miles	20
Walk No 9	BASINGBOURNE & ZEBON 3 Miles	22
Walk No 10	CRONDALL & THE HARROW WAY 4 Miles	24
Walk No 11	HORSEDOWN COMMON & THE MAULTHWAY 4 Miles	26
Walk No 12	CRONDALL & LEE WOOD 4 Miles	28
LOCATION OF WALK STARTING POINTS		16/17
POINTS OF INTEREST		30

Published by
ELVETHAM PUBLICATIONS
4 Eversley Drive, Fleet, Hampshire, GU51 1BG
www.elvethampublications.co.uk
elvethampubs@aol.com

FAMILY WALKS SERIES

Family Walks around Fleet, Crookham and Crondall   **2011**
ISBN 978-09553268-3-7
Family Walks around Farnham and the Hampshire Borders   2010
ISBN 978-09553268-2-0
Family Walks around the Blackwater Valley   2009
ISBN 978-0-9553268-1-3
Family Walks around Hook, Hartley Wintney and Rotherwick   2008
ISBN 978-0-9553268-0-6
Family Walks around Odiham and Beyond   2003

Great care has been taken to be accurate. The publisher cannot however accept any responsibility for errors which may occur, or their consequences.

The walk descriptions have been checked independently, but changes can occur. **If any problems are encountered on the walks, please report to the Rights of Way Officer asking for the problem to be cleared. Give a map reference if possible.** Contact details are:

The Rights of Way Section, (Hampshire)
Hampshire County Council, Mottisfont Court, High Street
Winchester, Hampshire SO23 8ZF
Tel: 0845 6035636
e-mail: rights.of.way@hants.gov.uk
web site: www.hants.gov.uk/row

ABBREVIATIONS

R	Right	SP	Signpost
RHS	Right hand side	S	Stile, kissing gate or squeeze posts
L	Left	FB	Footbridge
LHS	Left hand side	W	Waymark

INTRODUCTION

This new edition covers twelve circular walks in the attractive countryside around Fleet, Crookham and Crondall. It includes all the walks from the previous Family Walks book, which have been revised and updated. The usual format of the walk description and its accompanying map on facing pages is retained. The paragraph numbers correspond to the numbers shown on the maps. Points of Interest seen from the walks are described separately at the end of the book.

Starting points for the walks (where parking should be available) are shown on a map in the centre pages of the book. However all of the walks can be started from any point on the walk and indeed for some walks alternative start points are indicated. Some walks may be started using train services to Fleet and possibly Winchfield stations or bus services to some villages. Information about public transport may be found at: www.hants.gov.uk/passengertransport, or from Traveline – www.traveline.info or telephone number 0871 2002323.

Ordnance Survey Explorer Maps 144 and 145 at a scale of 2½ inches to the mile show all the footpaths used in the walks in detail and allow variations in the walks should it be desired. The maps included in the book give adequate guidance but walkers are encouraged to use the relevant Explorer map.

Most of the walks pass close to public houses and some pass tea rooms where refreshments are available for thirsty walkers. Please ask the landlord for their permission if you wish to leave your car in the car park (and remember to use their hospitality). At the time of writing a number of the pubs were under threat, if you are relying on them for refreshment it may be advisable to check first.

In dry conditions good walking shoes should suffice, but wellies may be needed in wetter conditions. Dog owners must keep their dogs on a lead where livestock is present and should be very wary in fields with livestock and their young.

Some walks pass close to private houses - please respect the residents' privacy.

We would like to thank those local businesses who have helped to support this series of books by taking out advertising space. We would encourage you to use their services.

We are grateful to Bob Rose for inviting us to update the Family Walks series of books, his encouragement, guidance and support. Our thanks go to Ted Blackman for the sketch maps (based on out of copyright maps and path surveys) and to Judy Dawkins and Alison Callaway for checking the descriptions for us. Thanks also go to Wendy Nicholas, the Crondall Parish footpath representative for the North East Hampshire Ramblers Group, for her help and information about footpath changes. Also thanks go to to Phyllis Ralton, Fleet and Crookham Local History Group www.fclhg.hampshire.org.uk for clarifying information about Daphne Du Maurier.

Stephen and Pam Turner
August 2011

Cover photograph front: The end of the walk, Crookham Village (by Stephen Turner) - see walk number 1. Cover photograph back: The Authors (by John Turner).

Walk No 1   CROOKHAM AND DOGMERSFIELD

[4 miles, 2 hours]

1. Start from the Crookham Village WI Hall next to Crookham Street Social Club. Return to The Street and turn L along the road passing The Black Horse. Cross over The Street to the footway opposite and continue ahead. A few yards beyond Veronica Drive look out for a footpath signpost on the R. Turn R along an enclosed path, go through a small metal gate and follow the enclosed path between fields (ignore the path on the L). Go through a chicane, turn R through a gap and along the path on the edge of the wood. At a stile on the R, turn L on the track through the wood and over a sleeper footbridge to reach the road.

2. Turn R along the road, go over Poulters Bridge, bear R and soon cross over the River Hart. Pass Burnt House on the R followed by a footpath signpost. Turn R along the enclosed path to reach Crondall Road. Turn R along the road, go over Chequers Bridge* and pass the Exchequer. In 250 yards pass Stroud Lane on your L, and in a further 120 yards cross a bridge with white rails. Shortly opposite Brook House, turn L over a stile by a footpath signpost to Dogmersfield.

3. Go across the field initially with the fence on the L. Continue ahead over a stile (with a waymark) and footbridge to the next field. Head for its RH corner, cross the stile by an iron gate (can be very muddy), turn R along a wide track between fences. At the front of the bungalow, turn R along the metalled track to reach the road.

4. Turn L along the road to Dogmersfield and shortly turn R at a footpath signpost. Follow the enclosed path by a stream, over a stile and continue on the enclosed path leading to a gap. Cross the wide track and keep ahead with the River Hart on the L and a fence and then trees on the R. Enter a large field, turn R along the RH field edge. At the oak tree on the R, keep ahead across the field aiming for the LH end of a line of trees. Cross the footbridge and stile to the next field, turn half L diagonally across the field (go round the LH edge of the field if wet) and over a stile and footbridge to reach Hitches Lane.

5. Cross the road carefully, turn L along the footway and in 50 yards turn R over a stile by a gate and footpath signpost. Follow the LH field edge; leave the field by a gap next to an old stile, turn R along the track and in 400 yards at the end of a field, turn R along a path between hedges. In 100 yards, turn L, with a copse on the right, and in a further 100 yards turn L along the LH edge of the field. At a stile and turn diagonally half R across the next field to return to the start.

* Note. The walk can be started from the canal side car park.

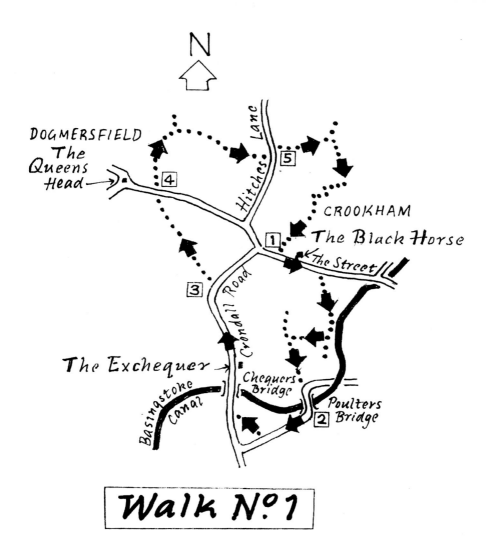

Walk Nº 1

Walk No 2   BEACON HILL & EWSHOT

[4 miles, 2 hours]

1. Start from Crookham War Memorial Hall opposite The Wyvern. Go along the RH footway of Sandy Lane, after 400 yards opposite Tweseldown Road, turn R at a footpath signpost. Follow the main path through the wood. Bear R at a Y-junction and go along the path with the field on the L. At the culvert, turn L along the enclosed path that shortly opens up to a track and reaches a road.

2. Turn R along the road and 50 yards beyond the last houses, at a 2 fingered footpath signpost, turn L. Go over a small footbridge and keep straight on through a copse, ignoring the path on the R. Keep ahead, ignoring all side paths. Pass under some overhead power cables and in about 200 yards go L on a faint path to enter the woodland by a large ash tree. Look out for a low waymark post on the R. Keep ahead on the clear path through the wood to reach Tadpole Lane at a footpath signpost.

3a. Turn L along the road and in a few yards, turn R over a stile opposite a footpath signpost *1. Go along the RHS of the field, over a stile and keep to the field edge (can be wet). Cross another stile, and continue through the paddocks keeping to the RHS to the field corner. Cross a stile and go along the drive passing houses to reach Beacon Hill Road. Turn R up the hill for 10 yards and with extreme caution cross the busy road to a gap in the trees. Go through the conifers for 100 yards and then turn R up a very steep wide track up Beacon Hill.

3b. Turn L along the road to it's junction with Beacon Hill Road. Cross the road with great care onto a path by a barrier. In a few yards, at a crossroad of tracks, turn R onto a wide very steep track up Beacon Hill.

4. At the top of the hill, fork R on a grass track. In due course continue parallel to the road to reach a cattle grid and kissing gate (for Caesar's Camp, turn L through the kissing gate onto a track for about a mile). Turn R to go through a metal barrier to the road.

5. Cross Beacon Hill Road with care, to the bridleway signpost diagonally L opposite. Follow the track through the wood and descend along the road passing houses and The Windmill. Continue down the hill; at the T-junction, turn R at Tadpole Lane by Ewshot Village Hall. In 30 yards, turn L at a footpath signpost and go through the car park *2.

6. Go to the L of the tennis court and through a gap in the hedge; keep along the LHS of the field, through some trees and turn half R across the next field and descend on a grass path to a gap in the trees. Cross the ditch by a footbridge and turn half L on a path passing a large oak tree in mid-field. Shortly fork R on the path and continue to the LH corner of the field to the two fingered signpost (you have now reached the same route as the outward journey).

7. Turn R along the road and opposite the "Wakefords Park" sign, turn L along the track through the wood. Turn R at the culvert and L along Sandy Lane to return to the start.

*1 Note. In summer month this path may be difficult to use because of the density of the stinging nettles. It may be preferable to follow the description at 3b.

*2 Note. The walk can be started from here.

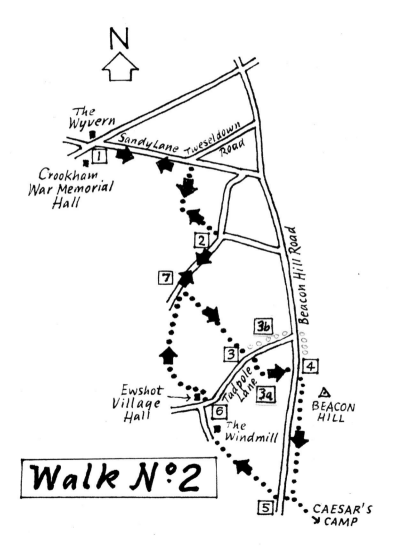

Walk N°2

Walk No 3 BRAMSHOT & MINLEY

[4 miles, 2 hours]

1. Start from Bramshot railway bridge opposite the sign to Fleet Pond on the A3014 Cove Road, Fleet (Car parking is possible over the bridge). Carefully cross the A3014 (watch for traffic) and turn R for 100 yards along the LHS of the road to a footpath signpost. Follow the path L through the wood with Little Coneyhurst fence on the R. At a waymark post, bear R along a gravel path through a tree screen to cross a track. Go ahead on the earth track across a large field to join the road at Great Bramshot Farmhouse.

2. Turn L along Bramshot Lane and in due course go through a gap by a metal gate in the road. At a wooden fence at the base of an embankment, bear R along the track. Pass under the M3 access road, turn L and follow the track to reach Minley Road via a metal barrier.

3. Turn L over the M3 bridge on the LHS of the road and turn L down a road crossing to the footway opposite. Shortly cross back over the road, pass wooden posts and go along a cycle and footway. With care cross the road by a 20 mph sign, to wooden barrier and turn L on a tarmac path that bears R and runs parallel to Minley Road. Pass the Crown & Cushion on the L * and in 250 yards reach a metal barrier and bridleway signpost on the L.

4. Turn L by the barrier, carefully cross the road to the bridleway signpost opposite. Go along the track with cottages on the R and through a gap by a metal gate. Keep ahead on the track ignoring all side turnings. The track becomes a grass path (Look out for Minley Manor on the R through the trees - without leaves in Autumn and Winter). Turn L at a waymark post and soon R along an enclosed path that opens up and has a tall hedge on the R. Pass under a large pylon and keep ahead on a grass track still with the hedge on the R. Leave the field by its RH corner to reach a wide gravel track.

5. Turn L along this track passing "Out of Bounds to Troops" signs on the R. Cross a bridge over the M3, at the end of the wooden fence on the L, turn L along a track and in ½ mile pass Bramshot Farm on the R to shortly reach the footpath used on the outward journey. Turn R on the gravel path through the wood and in a few yards at a footpath signpost, turn L on a path through the trees to pass the Little Coneyhurst fence on the L. Turn R along the A3014 (watch traffic) to return to Bramshot railway bridge.

*Note. If using the Pub car park as your starting point, please seek Landlord's permission.

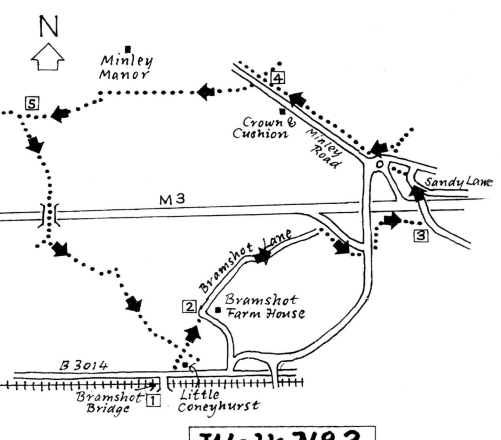

N

Minley Manor

5

Crown & Cushion

4

Minley Road

Sandy Lane

M3

3

Bramshot Lane

Bramshot Farm House

2

B 3014

Bramshot Bridge   1   Little Coneyhurst

Walk Nº 3

Walk No 4   ITCHEL MILL SPRINGS

[4 miles, 2 hours]

1. Start from Crookham Wharf car park, Basingstoke Canal. Turn R to go along Crondall Road over Chequers Bridge, in 100 yards at Crondall House fork L at the waymark post along the track between houses that leads to a lane. Turn R along this lane and shortly turn L along Crondall Road. In 200 yards turn R along the second lane by a byway signpost opposite a house called Two Ponds. Just before the farm, fork L at a waymark post and continue along the lane (can be muddy) that leads to a track through a wood. Cross the golfers' path, bear slightly R and continue along the lane passing Bowenhurst Golf Club on the L. Keep ahead on the metal road and just beyond Bowenhurst Farm & Stud on the L, take the grass track on the LHS of the road. At the Plough Garage, turn R along Mill Lane. At the end of the lane, by a white post, go through the trees to reach the A287.

2. Carefully cross the busy A287 to the footpath signpost diagonally R opposite, to the R of Itchel Pumping Station. Take the enclosed path, in 50 yards at an iron gate in a wire fence to the L, turn R at a waymark post along the path with the mill pond on the L (often dry). At Itchel Mill Springs (also often dry) turn L and shortly cross a stile. Keep along the LHS of the fields and in the second field, cross the stile and continue ahead on an enclosed path. Keep ahead along a line of oak trees, over two stiles to join Hyde Lane.

3. Turn L along the Hyde Lane, and at the road junction turn L along the Bowling Alley (or keep ahead for 220 yards to visit The Horns). In about 250 yards, turn R at a footpath signpost, through a kissing gate and along the RHS of the meadow. Go through a kissing gate in the corner and carefully cross the A287, go 25 yards to the R to the footpath signpost close to the road junction sign. Turn L and go along the enclosed path to reach Crondall Lane.

4. Turn L along the road and 80 yards beyond a house called Triggs, turn R at a footpath signpost, go through a kissing gate into a field. In 30 yards turn L at a waymark post. Do not cross the River Hart but go along the LH bank of the river and through two adjacent kissing gates. Go along the RHS of a large meadow, cross a stile and continue on the RHS of the next meadow. Just before the last overhead power cables, look out for and cross a footbridge on the R. Turn L and go along the river bank. In about 100 yards when the river turns L, bear half L across the meadow. Go through the kissing gate, along a boardwalk and through a second kissing gate. Go up the hill to the L of the pill box blockhouse and head for a kissing gate by the footpath signpost. Go over Poulters Bridge, turn L and along the towpath to return to the start.

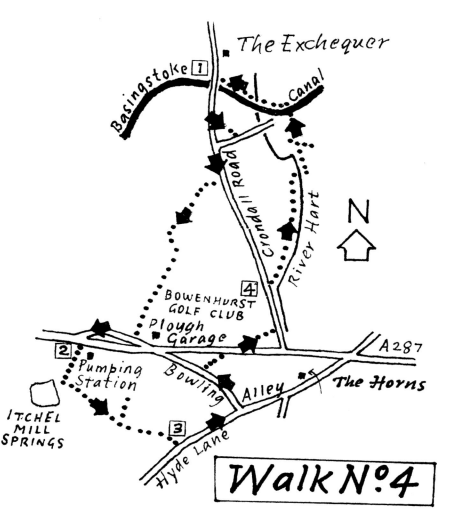

The Exchequer

Basingstoke [1]

Canal

Crondall Road

River Hart

N

[4]
BOWENHURST
GOLF CLUB
Plough
Garage

A287

[2]
Pumping
Station
Bowling Alley
The Horns

ITCHEL
MILL
SPRINGS

[3]
Hyde Lane

Walk Nº4

11

Walk No 5 CRONDALL

[4 miles, 2 hours]

1. Start from the Zebon Copse Centre, at the end of Danvers Drive, Crookham Village. Walk back towards the houses and turn R on the bridleway to the R of the tarmac cycleway. At the 3-fingered signpost, turn R over a stile and follow the path through trees with the stream on your L. Turn R through a kissing gate. Go along the LHS of the field and at the kissing gate, turn L over a boardwalk and through another kissing gate. Bear half L across the field for about 50 yards to the wire fence and then follow the River Hart on your R. In the field corner, turn R over the footbridge and then L along the LHS of a large field. Cross the stile and keep along the LHS of the next large field. Go through two kissing gates a short distance apart and go ahead with the River Hart on your L. Turn R at an old gatepost (waymark on other side) and go through the kissing gate to Crondall Road.

2. Turn L along the road (can be busy) and with caution cross the busy A287 to the footpath signpost opposite (definitely use the traffic island about 50 yards to your R). Go along the tarmac track to reach and cross The Bowling Alley (or turn L for 220 yards to visit The Horns). Turn R along the footway, at the sharp RH bend in the road, go a few yards along Hyde Lane and turn L at a footpath signpost along an enclosed path that leads to a large field. Go round the RHS of the field and turn L at the end to pass Lefroys Field houses to reach Pankridge Street.

3. Turn R along the road and just beyond the telephone box, turn L along Redlands Lane. At the last building on the R (surgery), take the enclosed footpath ahead, parallel to the lane. In 150 yards, look out for some steps on your L and cross the lane and a stile opposite. Go along an enclosed path between fields. Cross a stile and then two adjacent stiles to another field and bear slightly L across the field to a kissing gate. Bear L to cross a footbridge. Cross a stile and turn R along a fence. Just before the fence turns sharp R, turn half L across the middle of the large field. Pass two adjacent stiles and then cross a further stile and go over a footbridge. Keep ahead, passing three stiles to reach a stile by the A287."

4. Cross the busy A287 with extreme care to a footpath signpost and footbridge opposite. Go along the LHS of Peacocks Garden Centre. Cross a footbridge and a stile, bear slightly R across a field to a gap in the tree line. Bear L across the larger field heading for a stile about 50 yards to the R of Old Carpenters to join Dares Lane.

5. Turn R along the road and L along Ewshot Lane by Ewshot Lodge. Continue along the lane and in 300 yards, and at a RH bend look out for a footpath signpost by a green gate and fence on the L. Go along the path with the fence on the L, shortly passing a waymark post, and go along the RHS of the field. At the end of the field, cross a stile and go through Redfields

6. Carefully cross Redfield Lane to go along Watery Lane. Just beyond Stables Cottage, turn R through a gap by a footpath signpost*, cross a footbridge and through another gap. Cross a tarmac path and keep ahead on a sandy path with some houses on your R. Pass a footpath signpost and at a 3-fingered signpost, keep ahead on the enclosed track that leads to the Zebon Copse Centre.

* Note. At the time of writing the footbridge was under repair. Alternatively, continue along the lane and turn R over a bridge and then L onto the sandy path.

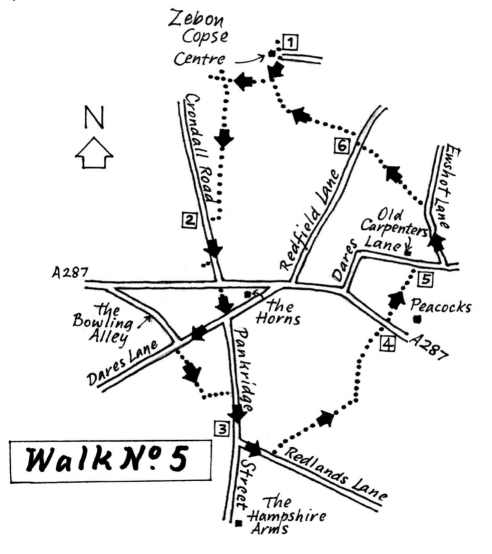

Walk No 6   BARLEY MOW & CROOKHAM

[4 miles, 2 hours]

1. Start from the canal side car park opposite the Barley Mow*, Winchfield. Go L along the towpath away from the bridge. At Blacksmith's Bridge, leave the towpath and turn L up a track and soon bear R on an enclosed path. Go over a stile by Double Bridge Farm and cross Church Lane to the footpath signpost opposite.

2. Go over the stile and across the large field passing to the L of a large metal pylon. At the next wooden pylon (with a waymark) bear slightly L across the field aiming for a stile by in a fence. Go along the enclosed path, cross two adjacent stiles and a further stile, go over a paddock to another stile. Turn R along the track between houses, turn L at a 2-fingered signpost, over a wooden farm bridge and through some trees. At another footpath signpost, go across a large field to a stile in its LH corner. Turn L across a small field, over a stile and sleeper footbridge, turn R along a track leading to Stroud Lane and reach Crondall Road.

3. Turn L along the road watching for traffic and in 120 yards cross a bridge with white rails. Shortly opposite Brook House, turn L over a stile by a footpath signpost to Dogmersfield. Go across the field initially with the fence on the L. Continue ahead over a stile (with a waymark) and footbridge to the next field. Head for its RH corner, cross the stile by the iron gate and turn R along a wide track between fences. At the front of the bungalow, turn R along the metalled track to reach the road.

4. Turn L along the road to Dogmersfield and in a few yards turn R at a footpath signpost. Follow the enclosed path by a stream. Turn L on the farm track over the River Hart and just beyond the bridge, turn R over a stile and along the track on the LHS of the field. Just before a metal gate ahead leading to a pond, go through a gate on the L and bear R along the RHS of the field. Soon cross an earth bridge on the R (by waymark posts) and go along the LHS of the next field. At a waymark post, follow a path through the trees by a small ditch. Cross a stile and turn L. Cross the ditch and go along the LHS of a large field. Go through a kissing gate and continue over two stiles. Continue through a wooded area to reach the road.

5. Turn R along the road and shortly at a RH bend in the road, cross carefully to a path to the RHS of the drive to Bridge House and join the canal towpath. Turn R along the towpath to return to the Barley Mow for a well earned pint!

* Note. Please ask the Landlord's permission if you use the pub car park.

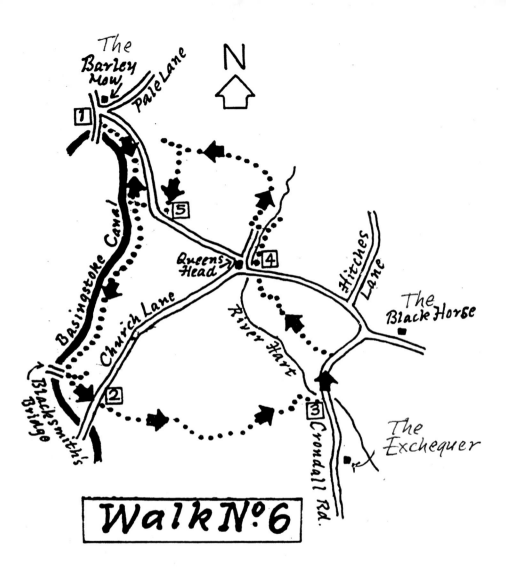

Walk Nº 6

The Barley Mow

The Hurst, Winchfield, Hants, RG27 8DE   Tel: 01252 617490
E-mail: thebarleymow@yahoo.co.uk   Web: www.barley-mow.com

Excellent reputation for food and cask marque real ales, warm
and friendly atmosphere, children and dogs welcome
Please call, e-mail or visit our website for any enquiry and we
will be happy to help.

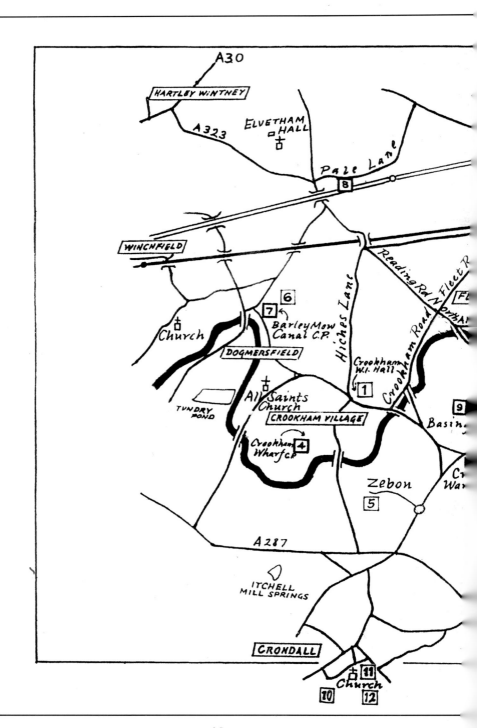

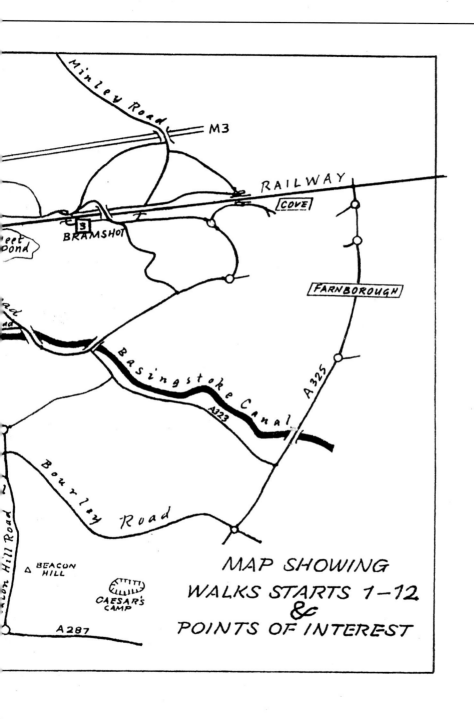

MAP SHOWING
WALKS STARTS 1-12
&
POINTS OF INTEREST

Walk No 7   WINCHFIELD & DOGMERSFIELD CHURCHES

[4 miles, 2 hours]

1. Start from the Barley Mow canal side car park, opposite the Barley Mow*, Winchfield. Turn R along the towpath under Barley Mow Bridge. At the next bridge (Stacey's Bridge), go R up the steps, turn R through the kissing gate and across the field to the stile opposite. Go ahead through the wood and two adjacent squeeze posts. Shortly go through another squeeze post and along the LHS of the field to enter the churchyard by a gate. Continue past Winchfield Church to the road.

2. Turn L along the road, ignore footpath signposts on the L and R. In ½ mile just beyond the S bend and Oak Hatch on the R, turn L at a bridleway signpost and along the track through Swans Farm. At a metal gate on the R, bear L along the track and over Sprat's Hatch Bridge to Sprat's Hatch Farm and Sprat's Hatch Lane.

3. Do not go along the lane, but turn R through a kissing gate by a footpath signpost and then bear L between fences (may be muddy) to join a driveway by a 2-fingered signpost. At the T junction turn L along the track to Tundry Pond. Go through a kissing gate and turn R along the edge of Tundry Pond. At the end of the pond, turn R along an enclosed path. In 100 yards, turn L over a stile to go over Blacksmith's Bridge. Shortly bear R along the enclosed track and go over a stile by Double Bridge Farm to reach Church Lane.

4. Turn L along the road (beware traffic) and in 600 yards turn L at a footpath signpost and then R into the churchyard and pass in front of Dogmersfield Church. Turn L to reach an enclosed path. Pass paddocks and the cricket ground to reach the road by the school.

5. Turn L along the road and in 100 yards at a footpath signpost, turn R along the path through trees. Go over two stiles and along the RHS of the larger field. Go through a kissing gate and maintain direction to cross a small ditch. Keep ahead to a line of trees and a stile on your R. Do not cross the stile but turn L along the path. Keep ahead through a line of oak trees. Beyond these oaks (may be muddy) and just before a metal gate on your L, cross a stile. Go along the RHS of the field (head for a metal water trough) and cross a stile to reach Pale Lane. Turn L along the lane and pass the Barley Mow pub, carefully cross the road to the canal side car park.

* Note. Please ask the Landlord's permission if you use the pub car park.

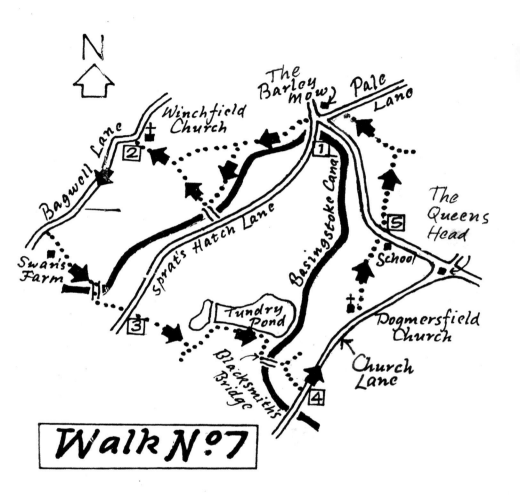

N

The Barley Mow

Pale Lane

Winchfield Church

Bagwell Lane

2

Sprat's Hatch Lane

1

Basingstoke Canal

The Queens Head

5

Swan's Farm

School

3

Tundry Pond

Dogmersfield Church

Blacksmith's Bridge

Church Lane

4

Walk N°7

Walk No 8   ELVETHAM

[3½ miles, 1¾ hours]

1. Start from the junction of Pale Lane and Turner's Green Lane (2nd on the L from the A323, park on the grass verge near the junction) north of the M3. Go along Turner's Green Lane passing the "No Through Road" sign. In ¼ mile turn hard L at the footpath signpost through a squeeze stile and cross the field to a gap in the hedge by a waymark post. Go straight ahead across the next field to the L end of a hedge behind "The Old Rectory". Bear R at the waymark post and follow the hedge to reach Home Farm Road through a gap in the hedge.

2. Cross the road to a footpath signpost opposite to the L and enter the field and cross a stile. Go straight ahead across the field (aiming to the R of two wooden pylons) to a stile in a fence. Keep ahead on a path through the plantation, cross a stile and bear L over a field to a stile on the R of a metal gate. Turn R along the track and L into the churchyard. Do not go beyond the church as the grounds are private. Retrace your footsteps to the road at "The Old Rectory".

3. Turn L along the road (beware of traffic) and go over Baker's Bridge. At a footpath signpost turn R along the track passing some cottages. Keep ahead along the RHS of two fields, pass through a gap in the hedge, turn R and follow the hedge on your R to the corner of the field.   Turn R over the footbridge and follow the wood on your L. In 30 yards at the corner of the wood turn L and go along the LHS of a large field. At Word Hill Farm barn, turn R to join a track.

4. Turn R along the track and keep ahead over a wooden farm bridge to Turner's Green. Turn R along the road and in ¼ mile turn L at a footpath signpost on your L. Go through a squeeze stile and across the field. Keep ahead on the track with the wood on your R. Enter a wood and shortly at a footpath signpost on your L, turn R through a chicane and bear R onto a driveway to reach Pale Lane. Turn R along the road and return to the start.

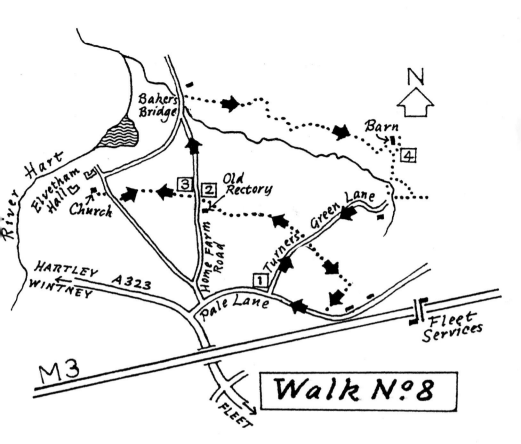

Walk Nº 8

Walk No 9   BASINGBOURNE & ZEBON

[3 miles, 1½ hours]

1. Start from Basingbourne Recreation Ground. Go to the end of the road (with the football field on the R) and turn L on the path through the wood keeping straight ahead through the pine trees to reach the houses. Turn R through the bollards along the tarmac path (Award Road) to reach Gally Hill Road.

2. Turn L along the road and pass the school, cross Ferndale Road and shortly turn R across Gally Hill Road to enter the churchyard of Christ Church. Follow the paving stones to the corner of the church, turn R down the steps on a grass path and then L along an enclosed path to reach Gables Road. Turn L along the road and R along the footway of Redfields Lane. At the roundabout, cross Brandon Road, turn L and continue on the footpath beside Redfields Lane to reach Watery Lane.

3. Turn R and pass a bridleway signpost and beyond Meadowview Cottage, turn R through a gap by a footpath signpost*, over a footbridge and through another gap. Keep ahead through a metal barrier on a sandy path (having crossed a tarmac path) with some houses on the R. At the end of this path by a 3-fingered signpost, go ahead along the enclosed bridleway. Cross over a road by the Zebon Copse Community Centre (walk can be started from here), pass a bridleway signpost and continue on the bridleway. In 250 yards, turn L to reach and cross the Basingstoke Canal by a swing bridge.

4. Go ahead down the track passing a 3-fingered signpost and Zephon House on the L (ignore the path on the R) and join the metalled lane. Shortly as the lane bears L, turn R at a footpath signpost, over a footbridge and follow the track through Peatmoor Copse. At the end of the copse, cross the stile and go along the enclosed path between fields. Cross a further stile and along the enclosed track to reach Crookham Street opposite The Black Horse.

5. Turn R along the road passing Crookham Village Stores. At Malthouse Bridge, go down the steps to the Basingstoke Canal, turn L under the bridge and along the towpath. At Coxheath Bridge, turn L up the steps to Coxheath Road.

6. Carefully cross the road and turn R over the bridge and shortly L into Wickham Road. At the end of the road, bear L and go between Nos 64 & 66 on a tarmac path. Cross the footbridge and take the RH path at the fork and go through the wood. This leads to a footbridge and Basingbourne, the start.

* Note. At the time of writing the footbridge was under repair. Alternatively, continue along the lane and turn R over a bridge and then L onto the sandy path.

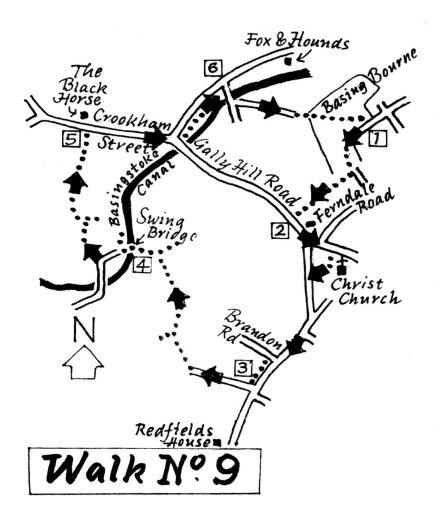

The Black Horse
Crookham Street
Basingstoke Canal
Swing Bridge
Fox & Hounds
Basing Bourne
Gally Hill Road
Ferndale Road
Christ Church
Brandon Rd
Redfields House
N

Walk Nº 9

Walk No 10   CRONDALL & THE HARROW WAY

[4 miles, 2 hours]

1. Start from Crondall Church. Go along Croft Lane, passing the church on the L, to Hook Meadow Recreation Ground. Turn R at the footpath signpost by a footpath map in the corner of the recreation ground. Go along the RHS of the recreation ground passing beside Crondall Village Hall and the bowling green. Join a tarmac path alongside a wall on the R, follow it to the road. Turn R along the road passing The Plume of Feathers and Crondall Stores, and continue past The Hampshire Arms. Continue along the road past the redundant chapel.

2. Turn R into Redlands Lane. At the last building on the R (surgery), take the enclosed footpath ahead, parallel to the lane. At the end of the wire fence, turn R along the RHS of the golf course. Continue along an enclosed path with the wire fence on the R. Turn R and then L following the wire fence. Do not go through the kissing gate in the corner, but turn L along RHS of the golf course to reach Heath Lane.

3. Turn R along the road (watch for traffic). At the T-junction, turn R and cross the road to the footpath signpost opposite, between hedges beside Cherry Bank. Go along the enclosed path and turn L along the road. At the next T-junction turn R along the road and at the footpath signpost on the LHS, turn L along the enclosed path between Nos. 26 & 27.

4. Shortly turn R then L at a waymark post by a metal barrier. Go along the LHS of a large field. Go through a gap and continue along the LHS of the next large field gradually going uphill. At the top of the hill pass but do not cross a stile on the L and continue to the corner of the field. Cross the stile in the field corner and descend by the steps to a narrow lane (the Harrow Way).

5. Turn R along the lane (beware traffic) and in 400 yards turn R at a footpath signpost by a metal gate and go along the enclosed track. Pass another metal gate on the RHS, but do not enter Barley Pound. Keep on the descending track which leads across open fields (ignore side turnings). At the end of the large field, pass a metal gate and along Farm Lane to reach the road at Pilgrims Cottage opposite.

6. Turn R along the road passing Hook Meadow Recreation Ground to return to the start.

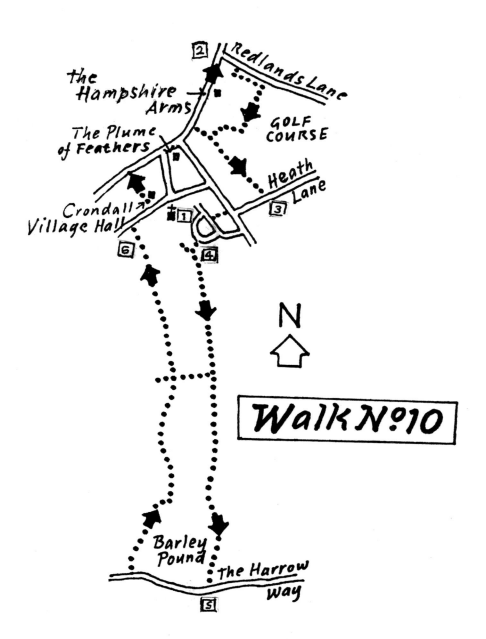

The Hampshire Arms

Redlands Lane

2

GOLF COURSE

The Plume of Feathers

Heath Lane

3

Crondall Village Hall

1

6

4

N

Walk Nº 10

Barley Pound

The Harrow Way

5

Walk No 11   HORSEDOWN COMMON & THE MAULTHWAY

[4 miles, 2 hours]

1. Start from Crondall Church. Go along Croft Lane passing the church on the L and Hook Meadow Recreation Ground on the R. Just before Farm Lane, turn R at a footpath signpost and go between a hedge and the tennis court. In a few yards turn L through a gap in the hedge and go diagonally across the field to its opposite corner to reach the road junction.

2. Go ahead on Well Road and in about 50 yards turn R at a footpath signpost, over a footbridge and along the LHS of the field (with a ditch on the L). Turn R along the road and R again at the T-junction for a few yards to a footpath signpost.

3. Turn L along the field path with the bank on the R. In half a mile turn R at a waymark post and then L at a second waymark post with a line of trees on the R. In about 100 yards turn R over a footbridge and then L along the LHS of the next field to reach a waymark post at the end of the field.

4. Turn L through the gap into another field and in 40 yards turn R through a gap by a footpath signpost and along the RHS of a line of oak trees. Cross a track, through a small gate and over a stile to enter Horsedown Common (may be muddy). Turn L and go through the trees keeping close to the LH edge of Horsedown Common. Descend and cross a long plank bridge and go through a small gate by a stile to leave Horsedown Common. Follow the path through the copse that bears R at its end, then turn L between two trees (waymark post behind right hand tree) and go along the RHS of the field to a footpath signpost in the field corner.

5. Turn L along The Maulthway that descends between steep banks and in due course becomes a metalled road. Continue along the road and fork R at a junction passing Jonathan's Kiln Cottages where a road joins from the L. Continue on this road and at the T-junction turn L down Well Road. At the next road junction, go through the gap on the R by a footpath signpost and along the LHS of the field. Continue ahead through a gap between two trees to the next field. In the field corner, turn L over a stile, down the steps and then R along the road that leads to The Plume of Feathers. Turn R along Church Street to return to the start.

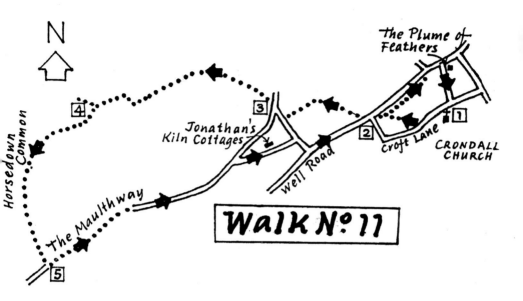

Map labels: N, Horsedown Common, The Maulthway, Jonathan's Kiln Cottages, Well Road, Croft Lane, Crondall Church, The Plume of Feathers, 1, 2, 3, 4, 5

Walk Nº 11

THE PLUME OF FEATHERS

SET IN THE PICTURESQUE VILLAGE OF CRONDALL
A 16TH CENTURY COACHING INN
ONE OF THE OLDEST PUBS IN ENGLAND

COMFORTABLE, FRIENDLY LOCALS BAR
LOG BURNING STOVE
OAK-BEAMED CANDLE-LIT RESTAURANT
FULL À LA CARTE MENU
FOOD SERVED LUNCH AND DINNER
SEVEN DAYS-A-WEEK

The Borough, Crondall, Hants GU10 5NT

TEL: 01252 850245
WEB: WWW.PLUMECRONDALL.CO.UK

Walk No 12   CRONDALL & LEE WOOD

[4 miles, 2 hours]

1. Start from Crondall Church. Go along Croft Lane passing the church on the L and Hook Meadow Recreation Ground on the R. At the sharp RH bend in the road, go ahead on the track (by a footpath signpost and metal gates) and in a few yards turn L at a waymark post by the barns. After ¼ mile, turn R along the track (ignoring the track ahead) that leads to and then through Lee Wood. After the wood, keep along the RHS of the field on a track that re-enters another wood and passes some houses and Swanthorpe House to reach a lane.

2. Turn R along the lane and shortly at a T-junction, turn R along the road (beware traffic). Pass Montgomery's Farm and in ¼ mile just beyond the spinney on the R, turn R through a gap by a footpath signpost and go along the LHS of a large field on a path that runs parallel to the road. In the far RH field corner, turn L through a gap onto the road.

3. Turn R along the road and in about 30 yards look out for a footpath signpost in the trees and turn R. In a few yards bear L at a waymark post in the copse. Follow the path through the copse that runs parallel to the road. At the end of the copse, turn R at a 2-fingered footpath signpost and go along the RHS of a large field. In the field corner enter Lee Wood between two posts and take the path that runs close to the RH edge of the wood. On meeting a wide track, turn L along the track (used on the outward journey).

4. Just before leaving Lee Wood, turn L on a path and in 25 yards at a waymark post bear R (do not take the path ahead) and leave the wood. Go to the R of a small tree on a path between two large fields. At the end of the large field, pass to the LHS of the barns and go ahead along Croft Lane to the church. If desired, turn L along Church Street to The Plume of Feathers for refreshments.

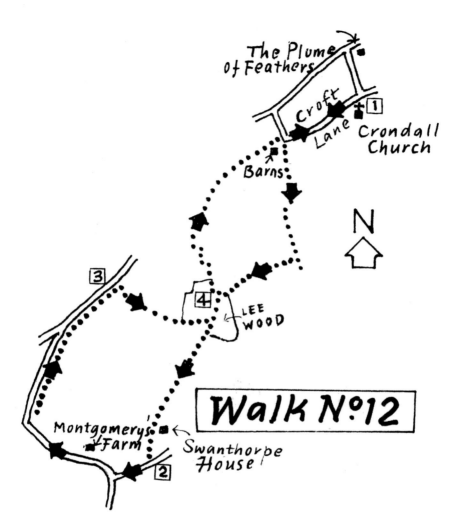

The Plume
of Feathers

Croft

Lane

Crondall
Church

1

Barns

N

3

4

LEE
WOOD

Walk Nº12

Montgomerys
Farm

Swanthorpe
House

2

29

POINTS OF INTEREST

Basingstoke Canal

Basingstoke Canal was completed in 1794. By the 1960s the canal was semi-derelict, but was restored as a public amenity following a campaign by the Surrey & Hampshire Canal Society. Crookham Wharf by the Chequers Bridge is now a car park, but it was once used to trans-ship coal and timber. Baseley's and Stacey's Bridges were named after local farming families. The Swing Bridge at Zebon Copse, Crookham is the only remaining one of its type on the canal.

(Walk Nos. 1, 4, 6, 7 & 9)

Caesar's Camp

Caesar's Camp is a pre-Roman Iron Age Hill Fort dating from about 500 BC. It lies about 590 ft above sea level and covers about 25 acres at the end of a steep-sided spur projecting from a gravel plateau. The fort is a natural strong point protected by the steep sides of the spur fortified by double banks and a deep ditch at the neck of the spur. These features have survived for 2,500 years and are clearly visible from the modern track entering the western end of the fort. The hill fort commands a magnificent view: Farnborough Airfield, Long Valley, Farnham and Aldershot; more distantly: the Hog's Back, Guildford Cathedral, Crooksbury Hill, Hindhead and to the north the Thames Valley and beyond with the Chobham Ridges to the north east.

(Walk No 2)

Crondall

Barley Pound was a small bailey and motte castle erected by a baron in the lawless times of King Stephen early in the 12th century. Only the earth banks remain in private ownership. Roman villa pavements were found nearby, but are no longer visible.

(Walk No 10)

Crondall Church All Saints dates from about 1170 and replaced an earlier Saxon church from King Alfred's time if not earlier. The font in the church is possibly Saxon and the three doorways are Norman. Originally there was a tower over the chancel arches, but the tower's weight and subsidence cracked the walls; buttresses were added in 1556 to shore up the tower. The leaning buttresses remain, but the old tower was removed in 1657. The present tower was built in 1659 costing £428. On the side of the entrance porch are several crosses supposedly etched by Crusaders before their long medieval journey.

(Walk Nos 10 & 12)

Harrow Way is a prehistoric trade route from Kent to the West Country. It pre-dates Roman times, being in use in the Iron Age and probably much earlier. Generally the Harrow Way follows the crest lines of hills and only descends to cross rivers. The section south of Crondall is a minor road through Dippenhall and Well and gives splendid views and a sense of antiquity.

(Walk No 10)

Itchel Mill was recorded in the Domesday Book in land held by the Bishop of Winchester. The mill used water from the Itchel Mill Springs and survived until about the 1850s. The mill pond and traces of mill race and Itchel Mill Springs may still be seen from the public footpath alongside. There are two artesian wells by the springs; water is siphoned from them to a deeper well at Itchel Pumping Station which since early in the 20th century has fed the local water supply.

(Walk No 4)

Maulthway is another prehistoric route used eventually by drovers taking their livestock to London. Its name is derived from Mault the Welsh word for sheep. The Maulthway branches off the Harrow Way close to the Chequers Inn at Well and goes down a sunken lane beside Horsedown Common and Swanthorpe Farm.

(Walk No 11)

Crookham

Christ Church, Crookham Parish Church was built with funds raised by public subscription and the support of Charles Lefroy, whose family had inherited Itchel Manor, Crondall in 1818. Land was bought in Gally Hill when there were few houses nearby. The first stone was laid in March 1840 and the church was consecrated by Henry Summer, Bishop of Winchester on 31 August 1841. Anthony Cottrell Lefroy was the first curate of the new church and parish of Crookham-cum-Ewshot. Soon a group of large family houses were built around the church mainly by friends of the Lefroy and Dyson families. This gave rise to the name Church Crookham. Anthony Lefroy built the parsonage and next a school opened in 1843. The original school was set back from Gally Hill Road. Following a diphtheria epidemic in the winter of 1893-94, the school was closed and a new, enlarged school was opened in October 1894. Finally another building was erected in front of the school and dedicated by the Bishop of Guildford in 1911. The Lefroys also built the Wyvern Inn in 1854, its sign is taken from the Lefroy crest. So the Lefroys, who were Protestant French Huguenots, gave rise to the quintessential English village based on a church, pub and school!   (Walk No 9)

Daphne DuMaurier lived in a house called Grey Friars, and at one time The Gables in 1938, during which time she completed the novel "Rebecca". The house, now demolished, stood in what is now Gables Road, Church Crookham. A number of road names in Zebon Copse housing estate have Du Maurier connections.   (Walk Nos. 5 and 9)

Redfields House was built in 1879. Mr Arthur Brandon a brewer from London, moved to Redfields House in 1896. He started the only successful commercial tobacco crop grown in this country which lasted for over 40 years until his death in 1937. The tobacco was grown in Barn Field, Crookham; the leaves were dried and cured in sheds on a site now occupied by light industry at Redfields Park. Stevens & Sons of Salisbury sold Blue Pryor cigarettes made from these leaves. Packets of these cigarettes contained cards showing the tobacco process in Crookham. This unique enterprise is commemorated in the names of Blue Pryor Close and Barn Field Close in the nearby Zebon Copse housing estate. During the Second World War, Redfields House was used as an Officers' Mess and subsequently a Conference Centre; it is now the new home for St Nicholas' School.   (Walk No 9)

Dogmersfield

Dogmersfield Church The first church, probably of Saxon origin, was close to Dogmersfield House in Dogmersfield Park and had been replaced by a Norman church which survived until 1806. Its ruins are on private land behind Floods Farm, Chalky Lane. All Saints the parish church was consecrated in 1843 following its building on a site convenient to parishioners in the newly constructed village around the old hamlet of Pilcot. Several articles were moved from the older church including a small 15th century bell, a 1590 memorial brass to Anne Powlett - an ancestor of the Mildmay family of Dogmersfield Park, and a 1562 Elizabethan chalice.   (Walk No 7)

Queens Head at Dogmersfield is a 17th century coaching inn. A recent document on the wall records the arrival at the Bishop's Palace (now Dogmersfield House) of Catherine of Aragon. She met and subsequently married Prince Arthur, the eldest son of Henry VII, but he died in 1502. Soon afterwards she married his younger brother, who became Henry VIII in 1509. Catherine bore him no sons and her only surviving daughter later succeeded as Mary I. Henry VIII wished to be rid of Catherine, but the Pope refused to annul the marriage. This led to the break with Rome, the divorce of Catherine at Dunstable and the establishment of the Church of England.   (Walk Nos 1, 6 & 7)

Tundry Pond is 3ft to 6ft deep and is on the site of Tundry Green Common. It was enlarged in 1808 during the landscaping of Dogmersfield Park by Sir Henry Mildmay. In the mid 18th century it was known as Wale Pond. Young fry were hatched out at the nearby Sprat's Hatch Farm and released into Tundry Pond.   (Walk No 7)

Elvetham

Elvetham Hall Elvetham, meaning the place of the swans, was originally a Saxon defensive site on a clay hillock surrounded by impenetrable marshes. It was mentioned in the Domesday Book; Edric held it from Edward the Confessor in freehold and it was awarded to Hugh de Port by William the Conqueror. It has had many owners over the centuries and passed to John Seymour in 1426. To regain Queen Elizabeth's favour in 1591, Edward Seymour entertained the Queen and her retinue for four days at Elvetham. An ornamental lake was created on the River Hart for the occasion and Queen Elizabeth planted an oak tree which can be seen from the public footpath to St Mary's, the former Elvetham parish church. The house passed to Baron Calthorpe in 1788, in time it fell into disrepair, was restored but burnt down in 1840. It was replaced by a hunting lodge that was developed into the present mansion in 1860. The style owes much to the influence of the European travel of 4th Baron Calthorpe. Elvetham Hall was used as an officers' hospital during the First World War. The mansion is now a hotel.   (Walk No 8)

Hawley

Crown & Cushion has associations with Colonel Thomas Blood who lived at Minley Warren. In 1671 he nearly succeeded in stealing the Crown Jewels from the Tower of London. Although he escaped, he was later arrested whilst imbibing in the Crown & Cushion. This was commemorated by a topiary in front of the pub cut in the shape of a crown on a cushion, sadly no longer trimmed. Blood was granted a Royal Pardon and an estate in Ireland worth £ 500 a year. Who said crime does not pay!
(Walk No 3)

Minley Manor Minley, known in Saxon times as Mindeslei, had been an estate of manorial status for many centuries. The manor house before the present one had fallen into disrepair and the estate was bought in the mid 1850s by Raikes Currie a London Banker and MP for Northampton. The present manor house was built during 1858 - 60. The architect was Henry Clutton and the design was said to be inspired by the Chateau de Blois. The Curries were considered good employers and they made many improvements to the estate. The Manor was enlarged later and remained with the Currie family until death duties in the 1930s forced its sale. In 1936 the War Department purchased the entire Minley Estate, principally as a training area. The Senior Division of the Sandhurst Staff College moved to Minley Manor following considerable interior alterations and it was re-opened in January 1939 by the Duke of Gloucester. Finally the renovated Manor was handed over to the Corps of the Royal Engineers in May 1971. Queen Elizabeth II lunched at the Manor in October 1976 when she laid the foundation stone of Gibraltar Barracks which are on the opposite side of Minley Road.   (Walk No 3)

Winchfield

Winchfield Church St Mary's was originally built by the monks from Chertsey Abbey and has been in use since 1150. The nave, tower with 5ft thick walls and chancel are Norman; the porch was added in the 15th century, but the door is Norman. The belfry, with imitation Norman windows, was added to the tower in 1849. The font has an original Norman basin, the pulpit dates from 1634 with the nearby 400 to 500 year old pews. The chancel has a semicircular curved arch with chevron and other Norman ornamentation. On either side of the arch are 'squints used in pre-Reformation times for the Mass to be seen.   (Walk No 7)